Introduction

This comic book is dedicated to those whose worl

The book was created out of boredom and out of feeling
Places in the book are as they were in 2017 and 1850. I have done my best to reconstruct Victorian
Hollis Croft in Victorian Sheffield by using archaeological evidence, historic Ordnance Survey maps
and written records. Names and characters are products of my imagination
apart from Pablo Fanque (circus owner) and Madame Naomi (palmist) who are historical figures.
All characters are used fictitiously.

This book would have not happened without the help of many people.
I hope I haven't forgotten anyone. If I have, I apologise sincerely.

To the Wessex Archaeology team who excavated the site at Hollis Croft, thank you for all your
hard work and comradery. To everyone from post-excavation, reporting, illustration and archiving
archaeological teams, thank you for putting all the puzzles together.

To my friends who had to go through listening to me developing the story and the characters and
to those who were also exposed to reading the early material, I am not sure you've helped at all,
but thank you.

To Gavin Johnson, thank you for securing a chunk of the financial support for this book.

To Wessex Archaeology (as an entity), thank you for your support in a
form of another chunk of the financial support.

To Dinah Saich thank you for believing in me and for letting me go off-piste with publishing the
results of our excavation as a comic book.

To Polly Singer, thank you for saying that writing a comic book is cool
and thank you for introducing me to Hattie Earle.

To Hattie Earle, Callum Seymour and Frazer Hudson,
thank you for being involved in the first draft of the comic.

To Pippa Bradley, thank you for being kind and thank you for helping me write better.

To Karen Nichols, thank you for your endless enthusiasm and for having so much patience
with my unorthodox ideas.

To Caroline Budd and Andrea Burgess, thank you for all your support throughout the years.

To the Jewitt family (Penny, Chris and the boys), thank you for letting me read the amazing
Footprint Tools Archive and for making me feel part of the gang.

To Judith Winters, thank you for saying yes to publishing the book online at our very first meeting
and thank you for not giving up on me.

To Paul Rowland, thank you for being omnipresent and for being a good friend with Dave Howarth.

To Dave Howarth... well, if it was not for you this would have never happened. Thank you, Dave.

And thank you to Caroline O'Keeffe for rescuing me in all moments of doubt.

If you wish to see how this story looks as a real and actual site archive and you are reading this
book digitally, just click on X (You'll find them on the full splash pages).
or go to **https://archaeologydataservice.ac.uk/archives/view/wessexar1-309354/**
This will take you to and through a full archaeological report, illustrations and photos.

If you are reading this book as a printed-out version and wish to explore more about
Hollis Croft, the physical archive is deposited with Museums Sheffield under SHEFM:2019.13
and Sheffield Archives.

MR
Sheffield, 2020

The Dig

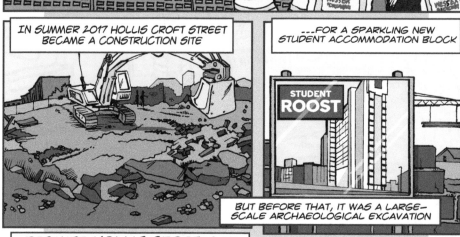

IN SUMMER 2017 HOLLIS CROFT STREET BECAME A CONSTRUCTION SITE

...FOR A SPARKLING NEW STUDENT ACCOMMODATION BLOCK

STUDENT ROOST

BUT BEFORE THAT, IT WAS A LARGE-SCALE ARCHAEOLOGICAL EXCAVATION

BECAUSE **HOLLIS CROFT** IS AN IMPORTANT PART OF SHEFFIELD'S HERITAGE...

...AND THE REMAINS WERE PRESERVED

The Cock

11

12

The Outside

NO-- NOT HERE.. MY FATHER IS GOING TO SEE US

HE WON'T COME OUT, HE'S WITH PABLO

PLEASE DON'T... SOMEONE ELSE IS GOING TO SEE US... I AM WORRIED

SO ARE WE GOING TO HIDE FROM THE REST OF THE WORLD TOO?

OUR WORLD IS SMALL... EVERYONE KNOWS EVERYONE IN OUR WORLD

THEN WE NEED TO DO SOMETHING ABOUT THAT!

The Crofts

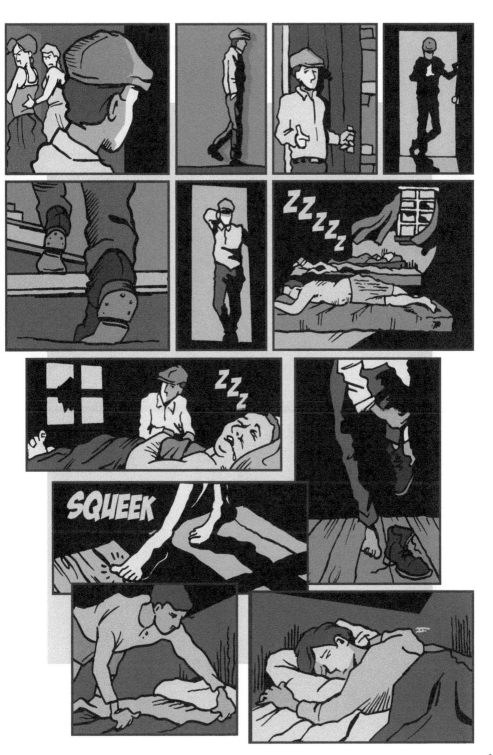

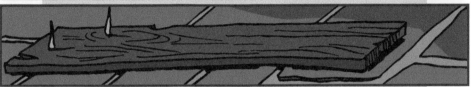

29

The Room

OH LOOK....I KNOW IT WILL COME TO YOU.... EVENTUALLY.... BUT JUST FOR THE RECORD

--- I SAVED YOUR LIFE... I WANT NOTHING IN RETURN FOR THAT LITTLE DEED... JUST STOP SAYING "NOTHING HAPPENED". PLUS I AM NOT ASKING ABOUT WHAT JUST HAPPENED. I SAW IT WITH MY EYES...

I AM ASKING YOU TO TELL ME WHAT HAPPENED TO YOU... FROM THE BEGINNING

YOU KNOW WELL WHAT I MEAN, I KNOW YOU KNOW I KNOW EVERYTHING ABOUT EVERYONE HERE...

THAT'S MY JOB!...

WHAT?.. WHAT DO YOU MEAN?

--NOTHING PERSONAL, JUST A JOB LIKE ANY OTHER... IT IS JUST THAT EVERY SO OFTEN I LIKE TO CHECK...

---CHECK HOW GOOD I AM IN GUESSING THE PAST AND PREDICTING THE FUTURE. JUST FOR MY OWN RECORD

SO--- CONNOR... OR SHOULD I, FOR THE SAKE OF MY ARGUMENT...

CALL YOU NEAVE?...

The Boat

39

The Finds

HOLLIS CROFT FINDS ARE IN!

OH GOOD... WE NEED TO SORT THEM OUT AND START PROCESSING THEM...

ANY GOODIES?

LOADS! THERE IS A MEDIEVAL COIN TOO!

A MEDIEVAL COIN? FROM 19TH-CENTURY SHEFFIELD??

YEAH... A LONG CROSS PENNY EVERYONE IS REALLY SURPRISED...

THAT'S A FAKE

URGH... REALLY?

The Circus

ONE SMOOTH MOVEMENT OR THE HORSE WILL SENSE YOU AND WILL NOT OBEY YOU!

OKAY... KEEP DOING THE SAME! PRACTICE... PRACTICE!! THIS NEEDS TO BECOME SECOND NATURE TO YOU! PRACTICE! PRACTICE!!

KEEP MOVING! ---KEEP GOING... STAY IN MOTION!

DONE FOR TODAY...
SEE YOU ALL LATER!

MR FANQUE... I... WE...
MY GIRLFRIEND AND I
WANT TO BE PART OF
YOUR CIRCUS SIR...

WHAT?..
WHO ARE YOU?
GO AWAY!

I AM... I KNOW HOW
TO MAKE THINGS...
AND SHE IS NICE...

WHAT?..
ARE YOU DRUNK OR
SOMETHING?
WHAT ON EARTH IS
WRONG WITH YOU?
WHO ON EARTH ARE
YOU?..

WAIT...
AND SHE IS "NICE"??
WHAT THE...?
HAHA HA HAHA
HA HA HAHA!
I DON'T NEED ANY OF
THAT...
ESPECIALLY I DONT
NEED "NICE"!
---"NICE"?
HAHA HA HAHA
HA HAHA!

--- YOU KNOW HOW
TO "MAKE" THINGS?

I CAN MAKE KNIVES
---I CAN MEND THINGS
ERMM
SHE IS GOOD ON THE
TILL...
WE WILL NOT BE
IN YOUR WAY
MR FANQUE SIR...

The Map

OH I SEE... SO THESE PLOTS ARE ACTUAL FIELDS AND THE STREETS ARE THE PATHS BETWEEN?

YEP... THE AREA ALREADY HAD COURTS IN THE LATE 18TH CENTURY. THEN IN THE 19TH CENTURY THERE'S A MIXTURE OF DOMESTIC, COMMERCIAL AND, I SUPPOSE, INDUSTRIAL... CUTLERY, KNIVES, FILES AND HAND TOOLS WERE MADE... AND, OF COURSE, SEVERAL PUBS!

WAT IS THIS THEN? CIRCUS TENTS?

HAHA... WELL, FUNNY YOU SHOULD SAY THAT, NO THESE ARE ACTUALLY CEMENTATION FURNACES... DO YOU MEAN THE TWO CIRCLES?

YEP...

YES, THEY ARE THE FOOTPRINTS OF THE TWO FURNACES WHERE IRON BARS WERE CONVERTED INTO STEEL. BLISTER STEEL. A SIMPLE PROCESS BUT A HARD WORK! THIS STUFF IS ALL OVER SHEFFIELD! CHIMNEYS EVERYWHERE... FURNACES. WE FOUND THOSE TWO AT HOLLIS CROFT. WELL PRESERVED. SHEFFIELD IS FAMOUS BECAUSE OF IT ...IT WAS LIKE...

HOLD ON... I HEAR YOU KNOW EVERYTHING ABOUT THIS... THANK YOU. CAN I GO BACK AND FINISH WHAT I HAVE TO DO?... YOU CAN TELL ME OVER A PINT LATER?

SURE... I GIVE YOU THE INFO... YOU BUY THE PINTS!

I'M NOT THAT DESPERATE TO KNOW THAT STUFF... BUT OKAY... IT'S A DEAL!

The Factory

AAAAAARGH!

DANG!

CLANG!

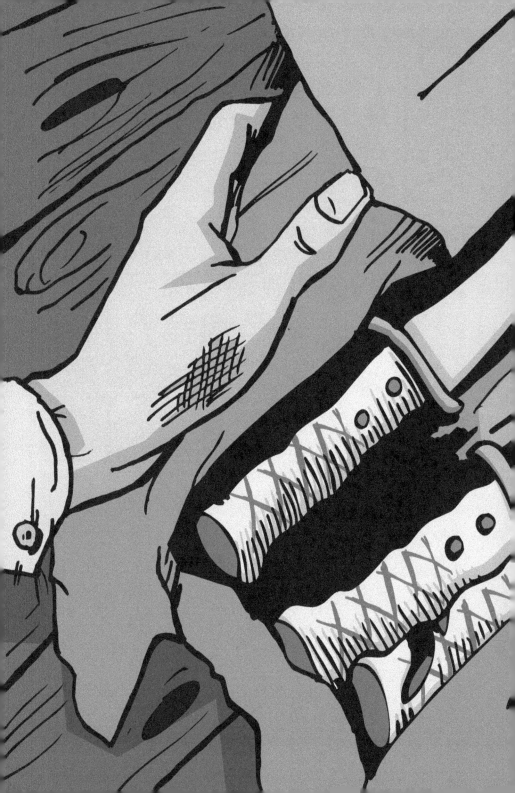

The Steel

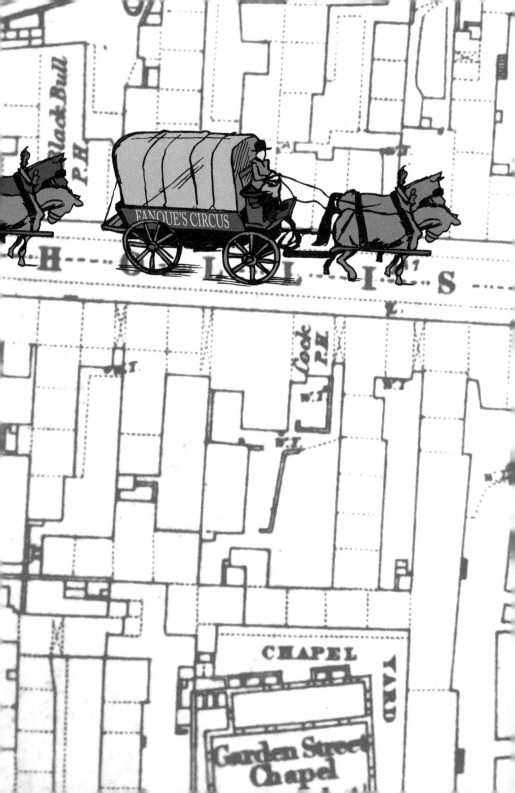

Black Bull P.H.

FANQUE'S CIRCUS

H · · · O · · · L · · · L · · · I · · · S · · ·

Lock P.H.

CHAPEL YARD

Garden Street Chapel

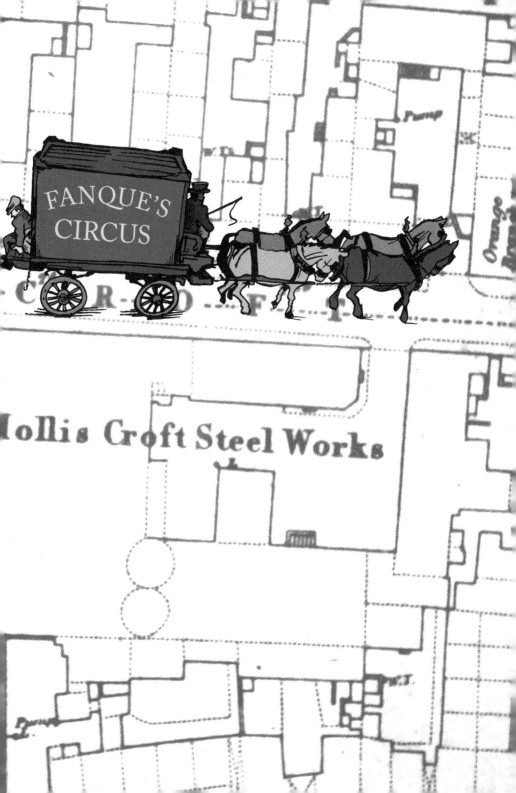

The Circles

The Author
Milica (Mili) Rajic is an archaeologist.
She reads an unhealthy number of comics,
likes prime numbers and odd things.
She lives in Sheffield and is deliberately getting old.

The Artist
Dave Howarth is a cartoonist and illustrator,
He buys and listens to an unhealthy number of
records, likes real ale and live music.
He's Sheffield born and bred and *is* old.

Lightning Source UK Ltd.
Milton Keynes UK
UKHW020411180321
380517UK00007B/97